It just is.

It just is.

Poems & short stories on soul love

Trinity F. Pasotti

Published by Tablo

Table of Contents

"And those who were seen dancing
were thought to be insane
by those who could not hear the music"

Friedrich Nietzsche

Ultimate Force

In pursuit of true love
I found eternity
I found beauty
I found universal oneness
and I found truth

That is how I know:
love is the ultimate force

Intrinsic love

It was the kind of love – the only real type of love –
where
"love" was sufficient
"love" was it
"love" was all.

Not love "because..."
No need for intellectual connection.
No need for mutual respect, commonality, shared values.
Love was all.
It needed nothing else.
Love was the beginning and the end.

It was totality.

Golden skull

The golden skull pulled you to me.
I didn't look into your eyes:
I had forgotten to look anyone in the eye for decades.
"Write your number," you said arrogantly
with the eerie deeply grounded yet subtle power
pulsating beneath the surface of your voice.
So characteristic of you,
you hypnotize one to do what you desire.
I wrote my number obediently.

The moment I first looked into your eyes
and found my long last home
was the first true day;
first day in many senses.
Under the starry sky, you triggered a shooting star
We hugged – total strangers, you and I –
so new yet more familiar than my own skin.
In warped time and space – an instantaneous apocalypse –
wall of fear and prejudice melted
and the shell of my identity made its first crack.

You flew in, I ran with my suitcase heart palpitating,
purer than the shaking tail of a puppy
at the sight of her long parted owner.
We kissed so passionately.
For being true to my heart and a small bit of courage,
the sky granted me five days of reasonless heaven.
Divine cares not for logic or reason,
it only cares for truth.
Only the mind fixates on delusional lies it tells itself,
"reason" is its tool.

This heaven was illogical. Ineffable.

You laid next to me, I pressed my ears on your pounding chest.
No rhythm, no chord, no note can put me in such sublime,
such trance.
I wasn't ready.
This love was too overwhelming.
I ran as a coward would.

Whereas the sky had only whispered to me all my life,
whisper so easy to ignore, easy to blend into the background to
point of oblivion,
it now screamed.
I tried to run, I tried to escape.
I reasoned, made sound arguments:
my mind fought hard.
But such is the effort of an ant grasping onto the sand as a
tsunami hits.
The divine omnipotence can't be grasped with such fragile and
limited monkey mind that is the human brain.
It's no battle at all.
And when the divine has decided on uniting two halved souls,
the decision is final.

I walked through hell.
The process of deidentification felt exactly as what it is: death.
How many times I died, I don't know.
Eight months felt like eighty years, eight lives, and
simultaneously, just an eight-hour nightmare.
Each time my shell cracked, it was crucifixion.

The human shell is no ordinary egg.
It comes in so many layers.
We spend our life adding yet more layers.

That is why whereas three-quarters of chicks hatch, almost all
humans die blind, never having escaped the protective darkness
of its thick, rigid shells.
As my own shell of ego cracked, I begged to go back and die
blind as everyone else.
The light seeping through the crack felt like acid burning,
piercing through my heart and electrifying my soul.
Its pain was too much to endure.
"Is this what I get for being good? The price of nobility is
excruciating punishment?"
I cried. I resented.
Silence was the reply.
Whereas its voice was so loud and clear when I ran,
now that I'm caught in pain, silence was all there was.

There comes a point in torture
when one is out of cry
out of energy to resist further
and simply detaches.
That is how it was when I finally surrendered.
"Take it all. All my human desires. All of my identity.
I fear nothing because I no longer exist."
I was down on my knees.
A stab here, a stab there: I no longer felt anything.
It was liberation.

I slowly peeled off remnants of my crack shells,
mesmerized at its thickness, at its many layers.
Inside the egg was a small piece of universe,
of divine,
of pure love.

What the fuck

and just as you begin to think you know what love is
to think you understand life, more or less
to think you've got a pretty good grip on this game of life

you come in contact with the eyes
of the love of your existence
and it fucking blows your mind

you had not a single clue about love
you had not a single clue about life
you had not a single clue about what you were doing

a moment of apocalypse
and your identity crumbles down,
soul you didn't even know you had ignites

in these first few days, weeks, even months
after meeting the love of your existence
all that comes out of one's mouth is
"What the fuck."

Run away with me

I want to stop chasing carrots
and explore the world with you
change the world
with you

Beyond body and mind

I used to think that loving one for one's mind
is the truest love.
If mind results from the accumulation of all of one's thoughts,
words, actions, and decisions,
I thought loving one's mind is loving one for who one truly is.

But if you transfer all your brain connections onto an artificial
mind map
and that mind map is placed in a biological clone of yours
how could I ever love that clone the way I love you?

I love you.
There is an essence beyond body and mind
I love your pure essence.

I love you if…

If you have nothing, I love you
If you have everything, I love you
If you are bad, I love you
If you are good, I love you
If you hate me, I love you
If you love me, I love you
If you destroy my life, I love you
If you lift me up, I love you

You see, my love for you "just is"
There is no reason, so nothing can change it

We are attached

The more I try to push away
the closer I'm pulled towards you

How is this possible?

There is a force beyond me, beyond you
that connects you and I
This cord is stronger than the silver cord of life

When we push away, the force only gets stronger
I can't waste any more energy trying to resist
the invincible pull

I surrender

Heart's desires, soul's desires

You could have "everything"
absolutely everything
but feel empty.
When you have everything,
the excruciating emptiness pierces even deeper.

You could have nothing
absolutely nothing
but feel complete.
When you have nothing,
it's more bluntly evident and amusing how all true treasures of
this world are free.

The key is in the soul.

No ego-feeding external success will satisfy your soul's hunger.
Only your heart can do that.
And you do not need to pay to fill your heart.

All you have to do is love.
Truly. Purely. Entirely. Honestly. Unconditionally.
With your whole heart.

Then whether or not you have anything,
you will be full
you will be complete.
All else is just bonus.

Brain love vs heart love - I

Love is so widely, universally misunderstood
because only very few will experience "true love" – heart love –
in a given lifetime.

In typical *loving with brain*, one first meets another.
Then through physical, emotional, intellectual, and situational
compatibility, they come to enjoy one another's company and
begin building shared experiences.
Through these experiences, a bond is created.
Where there was nothing initially, through bonding via shared
experiences, so-called "love" is created.

Both put in efforts to grow and sustain this love: it is very linear
and requires maintenance.
It needs to be fed.
After all, in the whelm of brain, "use it or lose it" holds true.
When one partner starts to neglect this love, the other needs to
feed it more to compensate. Eventually, the latter gets fed up
doing both parties' work. Then once no one is feeding this
"love," it starves and fades with time.
This type of love, *loving with brain*, is so intricately linked with
time and effort.
(Time x Effort) is directly proportional to growth, and when
effort approaches zero, this "love" shrinks to a point of
nothingness.

In contrast, in my love for you, in this *loving with heart*,
the love has always been, it is, and it always will be.
It is unattached to time: time and effort are both irrelevant and
unnecessary for its being.
It exceeds the concept of time.

Moreover, it is effortless, and in fact, tremendous effort is needed to try to prevent it. Of course, such effort can only lead to a temporary separation.

This *love with heart* existed before I met you, before I was born.
It has always been with me, so I was not "consciously aware" of it, just as we are not consciously aware of air until we are taught to intellectually conceptualize it.
That doesn't mean this love didn't influence me.
It had, even before I knew of its existence.

Then when I met you, it was unlike anything I've experienced…
because we didn't "create" love,
we simply "realized" what was already there.
Then everything – including my existence – began to make sense.
Like I've finally found my long last home.
The void inside me that I didn't even know existed, suddenly filled up completely.
And so, I just know with no doubt that this love will exist until the end of time.

Heart love requires no effort.
It requires tremendous energy and effort to try to separate, but as soon as one let go of such effort, we are instantaneously pulled back together.
There is an invisible elastic band between this love.

You see, the two types of love are completely different in nature.
Separate entities.
Abiding different sets of rules.

Brain love vs Heart love - II

Or as you put it, so eloquently:

"There are two types of love.
One, you go from 0 to 100 slowly, one by one.
You can reach 100 maybe in years.
Two, you get to 100 right away."

How come you knew all this back then,
when I had not a single clue.

Nothing mattered

Time did not matter
Language did not matter
Even character did not matter.
Actually, nothing mattered.

Paradoxical life

The more you know
the more you realize how little you know

The more you feel pain
the more you appreciate happiness

The more you care
the more you have to set them free

Note I wrote myself day before I met you

When the time comes to choose your life's work,
choose the pursuit of mission over the pursuit of pride

Whenever there is a transaction to be made,
choose based on the value and not the price tag

Whenever a decision is to be made,
choose the right decision over the easy decision

Every time you come to a crossroads in life,
choose the path of truth over the path of comfort

If fortunate enough to be offered even one,
choose love over ego

And in living life,
please,
Strive for adventure over perfection

Time & Space

Today I miss you
Yesterday I miss you
Tomorrow I miss you
There is no time, time is an illusion
in lieu of my love for you
Love somehow blinds time
Every moment is loving you
I am always with you and you with me
Love somehow blinds distance
What do I do now?
What can I do but love you

Cocoon

There is time for bodily growth
Necessary before the mind can develop

There is time for mind growth
Necessary before the spirit can develop

Then spirit, at last, starts expressing its true self
Only then can we remember our soul's raison d'être

Somewhere in history
We have suddenly forgotten about step three

We became a society stunted in the second stage
Too many of us died in the cocoon

We had forgotten
It's in our nature to fly

Soul love

I loved you, even before I met you.
Then when I met you – it was weird –
to finally see who this love belonged to.
It was so beyond the limitation of the mind
that it took me months to process and understand.

I now know why my love for you is so unconditional.

Because this is soul love,
the only "constant" lifetimes after lifetimes.
Soul love is timeless love. Unbreakable love.
The "variables" that change each lifetime, no, even within a
lifetime – appearance, abilities, mind, intelligence, social class,
values, personality, culture, religion, gender, family context,
possessions, beliefs –
none of these insignificant distractors matter.
They're so useless in the big picture.

The only thing that matters is your soul
and it took me so long to realize that
at the back of your car, under the starry sky
when I looked into your eyes
and pierced into the window to your soul,
that was the moment
I realized my love for you.
My soul recognized your soul.
There was a delay for this love to reach my brain,
but this omnipotent force was picked up by my soul right then.
That is why that moment is tattooed on my brain, heart and
being.

And that is why the "variables" – your form in this lifetime – are irrelevant to me.
You could have been of any ethnicity, any age, have any career, any appearance. I would love you the same.
You could have been crippled, and I would love you the same.
Then, I would have asked for the honor of helping you by your side until the end of this lifetime.
You could have been homeless, and I would love you the same.
Then, I would have felt blessed for the gift of being able to lift you up.
Heck, you could have even been female.
My sexual orientation would have changed to love you the same.

Our "relationship" in this lifetime also doesn't matter.
You could be a friend, a stranger, a romantic partner, family, or enemy of my family.
My love for you will never change, it simply can't ever change.
It just is.

That is how my love for you is unconditional.
Absolutely nothing matters in the face of love.
It's truly overwhelming.

What explaining this love feels like

Imagine a world with no real amusement parks,
only *virtual* amusement parks.
In this world, you and your friends go on believing that VR
rollercoasters – ones fixed in a single spot, mimicking the
movements by tilting the chair, blowing air, and using the
illusion of 3D imagery – are the real thing.
It's all we've known, so why would we question otherwise?
We haven't seen or heard of anything else, this is the only "truth"
we know.

The VR rollercoaster does provide some thrill.
It mimics a fall, you do feel a slight bit of stomach flip.
But somehow, it never fully satisfies you.
You don't know any better, so you think, 'there's just something
wrong with me.'
No one else seems to have any issues.
They look so thrilled by the VR rollercoaster.

Then something happens.
You don't know why, but one day, you wake up to find yourself
tied to a safety belt of a real rollercoaster.
No VR glasses. It's the real deal.
The moment it drops, you feel something, unlike anything
you've felt before.
The wind hitting your face, the feeling of weightlessness as the
chair drops, the intensity of sensation that every cell in your
body is acutely aware of:
it's incomparable to VR rollercoasters. Not even close.
You are utterly shocked. Disbelief. 'Such thing exists?
What have I been doing all this time, all that was fake.'

You go back to your friends, exploding with excitement.

"It's *different* from what we've all experienced, I swear by it!"

They think it's just a newer variation of VR rollercoaster. That's all their imagination permits.

And how could they imagine otherwise, when that is the only reality they've known.

You try to explain.

"Your heart feels like it's going to burst!"

They think: 'Obviously your heart rate goes up, that always happens, that's the point. What a drama queen.'

You say, "You get so sweaty, it feels like your stomach flips, the wind hits my entire body with full intensity, as if I'd fly right off if the safety belt were to break!"

They say, "I'm not discrediting your feeling. I see how much this has impacted you," they think, 'The sensitive ones always exaggerate. We feel the exact same thing, we're just not as sensitive, but it's the exact same stimuli.'

Frustrated, you scream, "No that's not what I mean! I'm the one who always complained that those VR rollercoasters are underwhelming, remember? I was always the calmest and least affected of all; I was the least sensitive, out of all of us!"

They think, 'You're just slow to realize. You're finally feeling what we've felt all this time.'

You feel like you're going crazy. You even question whether the ride really happened and whether you really are going crazy.

But deep inside, you know it was real.

It's the *only* real ride you've experienced all your life.

"No, I swear to God this is different. I *know* what you've felt - I had the same experience all my life, remember? This is 100% different, I can bet my life on it."

They think: 'How arrogant. Plus, sensations are subjective. How could you ever say what you feel is not what I feel? How dare you claim that your subjective experience is special while discrediting the rest of our experiences."
Last try. You say, "Can't you sense from my reaction, the magnitude of how this experience has changed me, that it might be something else?"
They respond, "Everyone reacts differently."

Perhaps there is nothing you can say,
no evidence that can convince them.
Perhaps there really are things that can only be understood through experience.

This is what my love for you feels like.
Everything I felt before: they were virtual in comparison.
Once I felt the real thing, I can never go back.
I can never be satisfied with the VR rollercoaster now that I've felt the real thing.
Incomparable. Ineffable.

It's the only true reality.
All else was artificial, virtual.
Nothing I say can convince them, but *I* know.
How can I be so certain this is the real thing?

It just is.
I just know.

Weak days

"Fuck this.
I can't do it anymore.
Stop testing me, I give up.
I quit this game.
I'm a coward.
I'm impatient.
I'm not courageous.
I'm not strong enough.
I'm a pathetic human.
I run away from emotions,
that's just what I do.

Like is okay
Love is not.

I can't.
My faith sucks.
This is the step where I fail.
Let me fail."

Ego - I

My ego wishes it wasn't you.
My ego despises you.
You represent everything my ego hates.
But my soul knows my heart can only love you.
It was custom-made for you.
It's not that my soul loves you, more that it was made for you.
Like not loving you is like negating my whole existence.
Like I have no choice but, as long as I'm breathing, to love you.

That's why my existence feels like suffering.

Tsunami

In a flat world, I escaped the emptiness by building a sandcastle
sandcastle, made up of my sweat, tear, and life story
sandcastle, that was my everything
sandcastle, that I thought was a real castle
I stood in awe of my creation
requiring just one more touch
it was at that moment I met your eyes

Seconds, hours. I don't know, it distorts
too short a moment regardless
that tsunami crushed my life's worth
wiped away my everything, my sandcastle
hitting me with truth that it was nothing at all
I am nothing at all
laughing at the insignificance of my life's devotion

I despised you
my mind saw you as the tsunami, the tsunami came with you
I wished I never met your eyes
to have lived a life in my castle, deluded of its illusory safe walls
you drowned me so effortlessly
the moment I stared into your comforting eyes, my home
the tsunami drowned me

Only when I cried enough, grieved enough
to crack open the shell of protection I layered to build my
sandcastle
did I see you for what you were
standing, not in front of me, but beside me
holding onto the remnants of your own wiped-away sandcastle
one that was even greater than mine had been

staring blankly at where the tsunami passed by

We stood together, in sublime
I didn't destroy you, you didn't destroy me
something beyond the reach of our small minds did
and without words
without sound
it somehow spoke to us
"Now you may build a real castle together."

Our hearts beat like it has never done before.

Ego - II

The ability to let go of one's ego
in its entirety
is the source of greatest power

How is it

Nothing in common
Such different worldviews
Such different personalities
Such different cultures
Such different languages
Such different backgrounds
Such different careers

You & I
We are so different
Yet how is it
that in the most intriguing way
our minds align
How is it that we are same
in a way no other two beings could be

How is it possible
that in such a short time
without any warning
you wipe away my life like a tsunami
Where have you disappeared to now?

How is it possible
To feel so far and simultaneously so close
under the same sky

Fire

My ego, rationality, reason
all of these vaporize in the heat of true love.
I just am.
In love with you.

Since the day I met you

My heart cries for you
My soul knows only you
My mind misses you
Every cell in my body longs for you

Not a single day
did I forget about you
Not a single moment
Since the day I met your eyes

The whole world

I see the sky
the sky is you
I see the mountains
the mountain is you
I see the sun
the sun is you
the world is you
you are my world

so in you
I live

without you
I cease to exist

How could it be any other way?

Love force

True love is the only force strong enough
the only bond unbreakable enough
to crack the shell of human ego.

I'm not saying this to be romantic, or expressive.
I'm not being poetic.
Rather, I'm just stating a fact, quite emotionlessly;
just being frank.

Because what are common drivers of human behavior?
Greed?
Need to feel belonged, cared for, accepted, and admired?
Craving to know and understand?
Pleasure?
Hope for the future?

Let me tell you,
no one is greedy enough, lonely enough, curious enough,
hedonistic enough, hopeful enough
to persist through the pain I went through
for those tedious, insignificant desires.
No one would kill their identity for those desires, no one would
die for them: death would negate those desires' existence and
pulverize all possibility for expression, so they obligate life.

Only love.
Because love is beyond self
solely about the other person
so through pain and death, it survives.
Only love survives death.

The only force that can be beyond one's existence.
The only force beyond this world.
Thus only love is strong enough to crack open the shell of
human ego.

That is why love is the greatest of all forces.
Do not confuse true love with "like," physical or mental
"attraction," sexual pleasure, need to feel belonged, friendship,
mutual respect or loyalty.
Those are all good things but are just different entities.
They belong to complete different whelms.

True love is so rare.
But once one sees, one can't unsee.

One soul

I am what you're not.
You are what I'm not.
Yet strangely,
we are made from one and the same.
Intriguingly,
we are one and the same.

That is why I can never not love you.

I wish you could see what I see

My love,
I wish you could see what I could see

You spend so much energy covering yourself in "fine" wrapping
You first spray yourself with TF
You then layer yourself with LP
You decorate your wrapping in RM
then you place it all in RR

You have truly placed yourself in the finest wrappings the world
has to offer
You pride yourself in your masterful wrapping

But my love,
Why do you forget the pure gold underneath the wrapping
Why do you blind the mesmerizing light radiating from the gold
Why can't you see, that gold is the only thing of true value

I fell in love when I peaked a small glimpse
of the pure you
the pure gold underneath the thick layers of packaging
Its blinding light put me in immediate sublime
The packaging is pretty, but it annoys me
because you too often hide underneath it

My love,
let me see the radiating light of the pure gold that is you
No packaging, no matter how grand, can ever compare to "you"
Please never forget that
No packaging can ever be worthy of you
So please, don't hide the gold with ridiculous wrappings

at least when you are with me
Nothing shines brighter than you

And my love,
please always remember,
you are not your packaging

You are immeasurably, incomparably more.

What this journey feels like

It feels like…

it feels like a dog locked up in a hard wooden box
the dog hears her pups screaming outside: they need her
the dog scratches the wall incessantly
just as a small crack is made
the dog is taken out and its claws are ripped out
placed back into the box

the dog now kicks the walls with bleeding, clawless legs
the pain is there, but it is not felt in the face of such desperation
another crack
the dog is taken out again, this time its four legs chopped off
placed back into the box
the dog now crawls to the wall
starts biting it, scratching it with its teeth
the dog is taken out yet again, and a mouth guard is placed

the dog lies down, legless, locked in its mouthguard
how could the world be so cruel
it lays there with burning tears

the intriguing part is
in that moment
the pain that the dog is suffering from
is not the bleeding site of its missing limbs
nor the small pieces of wood embedded in its face and gums
it's the ongoing cry of her pups outside the box she still hears
the cry pierces through her heart
that pain exceeds all
it anesthetizes the physical pain

if it were just for herself,
she would have given up a long time ago:
dying in the box would have been the easier option
but her pups await her

that is why
the dog crawls to the wall and now bangs its head on the walls.

Crack.
The box breaks down at last.
This is the moment the dog realizes the power of love.

The box opens, and with it, the dog awakens from the dream.
She opens her eyes.
Inside the comfort of a soft blanket,
wrapped around her four legs,
her pups lay snoring.
Their warmth on her skin never felt so real.

Nothing is the same from this moment on.

The question is:
Could one really say that the dream never happened?
The pain was felt – that was real –
the heartache was real, it felt truer than truth.
So could one really say that the dream didn't exist when it had
changed the dog forever? When the experience, the pain, and the
impact – they were all very real?

This time apart from you feels like a nightmare.
But it is a necessary pain.
To show what length I would go for you,
to show that love truly defeats all.

Fuck sanity

"What if I'm going crazy"
I kept thinking.
"Lack of insight characterizes delusional disorder, after all,"
I feared.
Delusional disorder, schizophrenia, schizotypal personality
disorder, organic causes of psychosis… I've considered it all.

The world sent me undeniable signs:
"It doesn't make sense, so it can't be true," I pushed away.
The heart sent me unavoidable messages:
"It's delusions. Hopeful thinking," I justified.
The dreams sent me clues and directions:
"It's all in my head. The brain truly is a wondrous organ," I
dismissed.

Until I realized,
I value freedom more than sanity.

Fuck sanity, I decided.

If I'm crazy
so be it.
At least I'm free.

Past life I: A life worth living

I was a young boy.
There is no memory of my childhood back home.
I was never happy there anyway.
Starvation, all struggle, no joy, nothing to live for.

Then, my legs rocking along with the waves of the ocean,
Dirty skinny legs, ragged up clothes,
I was being sent.
Unlike others, I wasn't afraid.
They were taking me away from no happiness.
Nothing to look forward to, yes, but also no longing for my life
back home.
That was the 12? 14? year-old me.
Sold and sent away as a slave.

I don't recall anything from the palace.
I don't remember any of the hardships.
All I remember is your beautiful eyes, my princess.
That's all I lived for.
Seeing your beautiful eyes, those eyes smiling at me.
Every day when I lay down to sleep, my mind would enter a
dream world, where you loved me back.

You were kind to me, unlike all others.
You never hurt me. You were never cruel to me.
It made me wonder at times – is it possible you love me too?
I shut that thought in seconds, a forbidden thought.
Impossible.
But even the moment of possibility is what made me go on
living.

When I aged – and I lived long for a slave, into the 70s – and I
became useless as a tool, as a slave
They threw me out.
But unlike other slaves, they also chopped off my legs and hands.
They never had such a loyal slave.
A slave who never complained.
Who was happy to serve. Who was happy to be there.
All other slaves would run as fast as possible if they were let out
of the palace, rejoicing at their freedom at last.
They thought I was crazy, "he would probably crawl back in,"
They laughed.
They thought I was crazy.
They didn't know that I lived to see the eyes of my love.

They knew I would return on my own will and beg to continue
being their slave.
So they cut off my two hands and my two feet,
Threw me away like used-up garbage in the desert sand.
This was the price of being loyal like no other.
I lay in the desert, unable to move, paralyzed.
Tears rolled down my eyes.
Scars all over my soul.

But at that moment, an intense ray of sunlight shone on me
its warmth surrounded me in bliss.
The sun was warm, the sun was you.
I was happy once again.
I was happy to have lived, even as a slave.
Because I have loved. With all of my heart.
I loved you.
Everyone in this life told me, whispered behind my back
That I was crazy
That my life was miserable, that my happiness was a delusion.

But I was truly happy, even armless and legless lying in the
desert.

When I woke up, the hypnotist told me "that wasn't a good life."
Just like all the other slaves told me.
Just like everyone thought of me in that life.
Why can't they see
I was truly happy
I loved.
Truly loved.
That made my life as perfect as any other.

Thank you my love.
Your eyes made this slave's life
Worth living.

In the sun
that is where
I remembered
I was always loved

How I realized I'm worthy of you

My love,
I'm not as strong as you
I'm not as smart as you, as wise as you
I'm not as powerful as you.
Actually, I have nothing and I am nothing.

But, my love,
the only thing I have – this love for you –
it's everything.
It makes me stronger than the strongest of warriors.
It makes me smarter and wiser than the wisest of men.
It makes me more powerful than the most powerful of kings.

Because
no warrior would die for more strength,
no wise man would die for more knowledge,
no king would die for more power.
But me? I would die for this love. I would die for you.
Only *I* would die for what I represent: love.

This is how I finally came to see
I *am* worthy to be with you.

It had been my biggest struggle: that you deserve a more
beautiful, more resourceful, more talented woman.
Someone who is your "equivalent."
Someone I can never be.

But, my love, I was wrong again.
Yes – I'm weaker than you, inferior to you in every way – but
one!

My love.
And that makes everything else meaningless.

If the time ever comes,
I would sacrifice my life for you.
I would endure any hardship, any pain, any struggle for you.

And with this love,
every day,
I'll try to be better. All for you.

Do not underestimate the power of love.
Love will give me everything, at the right moment.
Courage, wisdom, faith, strength.
Love will let me borrow all these.

I love you.
My love for you makes me the bravest of them all.

Quantum leap

Love is a quantum leap
surpasses what evolution would take millennia to accomplish
in an instant of an eye contact
it leaps not one, but multiple layers of being
it leaps not one, but multiple dimensions at once

one is left disoriented and confused

Eternal love

This love existed before I was born
But it will also exist after I die
That is how I came to realize
Death is nothing to be feared
It is an effective tool for my soul
A chance to restart
A chance to learn on a fresh new page, sans bias
Love is eternity, death is temporary

This love exists inside of me
But it also exists beyond me
That is how I came to realize
Self is a part of a greater oneness
It is an effective tool to help me focus on my part of the whole
A chance to contribute to the perfection of the greater oneness
A chance to experience oneness through diverse lenses
Love is oneness, self is a tool

This love exists in my current reality
But it also exists in all my parallel lives, it is a connector of time
That is how I came to realize
Time is flexible, non-linear
It is an effective tool, making expressions of free will possible
An enabler of change
A tool for observing, processing, and understanding life
Love bends time, lovers are time travelers

Do you see how this eternal love has opened my eye?

I love you

My love,
I hope you find your way back home
I miss you
I love you
Every part of you
No matter what you do
No matter what
There is no reason for my love for you
It just is
You are the one
The one and only
Lifetimes after lifetimes.

Free soul

Your free soul is what I fell in love with
so how could I ever take away any freedom,
imprison your soul in the name of love?

Seeing you lose your light because of my love
would be more excruciating than death itself.

My love,
My greatest wish is freedom for your soul
I could never let my love become any bondage.

Magic - I

Everything I cared about,
everything that mattered to me before I met you:
none of it matters anymore.
I'm so stubborn, it's almost impossible to change my worldview
but you changed me, every single day.
Every single day since meeting you has been paradigm shifts.
If that's not magic, what is?
If that's not love, then what possible force is potent enough to
ignite such grand changes?

"My love for you grows every day" is not an accurate statement.
My love for you exceeds the limitations of time, space and logic:
It was instantaneous love.
It always was. It always is. It always will be.
So a more accurate statement would be:
I uncover yet another depth of my love for you, every day.
It's but an endless sea.

I am nothing
but my love for you is everything.
It exceeds my existence.
My love for you is beyond my limited being.

Ego crack

Your existence tore open my rock-hard heart.
I can't explain it.
My futile attempt to understand it opened me to a whole new
world:
a whole new layer that has always been,
but I and most of the world had been blind to.

This is not just about love, in a traditional sense.
I don't want to call it "love"
– that term has been misused and misunderstood –
although this is the purest form of love there is.
However I call it, "it" tore open my heart, to reveal my soul.
It crushed down the "ego" wall, built from intellect, pride,
beliefs, preferences, tastes, personality, labels, identity …
the wall I worked so hard to build for decades.

The wall came crumbling down so instantaneously,
as if to laugh at my efforts,
show how small and insignificant I am,
and in contrast,
how omnipotent love is.

All this was somehow shown to me through you.
The kind of change and understanding that would take lifetimes,
it happened to me almost monthly, sometimes weekly.

It feels like I've lived nine lives since meeting you.

Truth

We tend to seek "truths" by searching externally:
a book that will reveal truths,
a person who will teach us truths.
When we do not find it, we search elsewhere.
We keep changing the "external" in hopes of finding the answer.

When in reality, one can see only to the limit of what one knows,
or is ready to see.
The eye and the mind are highly selective.

The thing is: truth is in all things.
In the sky, one can find the truth.
In a flower, one can find the truth.
In empty space, one can find the truth.

It depends solely on the eye of the observer.
One simply needs to become a person worthy of possessing a
further-seeing eye.

Once one possesses such an eye
it does not matter where or what one looks to
because truth is in all things
and so, truth can be found in all things.

We look for answers externally
when in reality, it's been inside us
untapped
all along.

Overflowing love is divine love

Soul love has a limitless source supply,
so soul love must overflow.
It begins with the beloved,
but soon, it overflows
to all beings,
to all things.

Once love fills the beloved,
one begins to find a part of one's beloved in everything:
in other people
then in animals
then in plants
then in rocks
then in air,
in warmth,
in water,
in earth.

There is a part of one's beloved everywhere
and love flows where one's beloved is.
That is how one comes to love all things.
Isn't that insane?
This love is so insane, so beyond logic.

And when the love has overflown everywhere,
the last place it finds
is in oneself.

It is this moment when one finds one's beloved in oneself
that this love transforms
from soul love to divine love.

Beauty

There is so much beauty in this world,
and I truly love all beings.
Even the worst of criminals.
The fact that they feel guilt is beauty.
Because they wanted to be good
but circumstances misled them,
and now they suffer in pain.

There is beauty in that pain.
They pain because there is good in them,
they pain because there is beauty in them.

Isn't it funny how you find beauty
in all things
when you are in love?

I know now

I can't bring my social status, intelligence or accumulation of
knowledge, wealth, and possessions with me when I die in this
lifetime.
But the choices I make: they do make a mark on my soul,
so they do follow me lifetimes after lifetimes.

That is why
knowing this now
I can never make a decision that would dirty my soul.
Not for anything:
death would be a better option than that.

One can fool others
but it can never truly fool oneself
and the sky is always watching.

Constants

In a world blinded by variables
The only constants:
Your soul
My soul
and that my soul loves your soul

Nature's beauty

It's odd.
Before I met you,
I looked out and marveled at the city lights, the grand architects,
the finest of human creations.

Now I marvel only at the limitless sky,
the trees, the mountains, the ocean,
and the bird flying right across them
the ultimate beauty, that no human can imitate.

Skyscrapers look so dull, so ugly, and lacking life.
It's annoying,
blocking our view of true beauty.

Love is free, free is love

Love is not bondage
Love is freedom

A purely loved soul is free to do whatever it wants
free to explore
the last thing a true lover wants
is for love to tie the other down
and lock their soul

I want you to be free to be you
I want you to explore this world

Just know that
during your exploration
when you need to recharge or you just want to rest
I am your home
that's all I am
I am your home
that is always open for you

That's all I want, my love
to be your safe place
nothing more

Through child's eyes

I used to know what's important,
we all did.
In the unfiltered, pure eyes of childhood,
we cared for the beauty of a flying bird in the bluest blue of the
vast sky;
we cared to wonder why stars in the sky exist and what is
beyond;
we cared to recognize that the same spiral of a pinecone is found
in the shell of a snail;
we cared to love, to hug a stranger, to cry when leaving a friend
we met for the first time just an hour ago.

We used to not care about the package, the outer wrapping, only
excited about the gift inside.
We would tear open the wrapping in a second, before we even
had a chance to cognize its appearance.

Look at us now.
How we grow blind, to spend our lives obsessing over & blinded
by the packaging that we never even end up opening the gift.

It's a funny world:
that courage is needed to tear open packaging of gifts.
Courage to do something that's utterly obvious.

How many shining gold stars are thrown away in unopened gift
boxes,
its beauty never seen, never appreciated.

Timeless family

I used to think that "I couldn't choose the family I was born into,
but I can choose the person I'll build a family with."
I was absolutely wrong, quite the opposite actually.

I believe I chose the family I was born into:
my soul chose my family in-between lives,
when I chose to be born again.
But with you, my one and only, it's not about choice.
You and I had no choice in this matter,
we were born one.
So we are the only ultimate, timeless "family,"
unchangeable lifetimes after lifetimes.

This can never change
because we were one.
This was chosen for us, even before our existence,
perhaps *right* before.

We just are.

Evil

there is not a single evil human on this planet:
only blind

no need for hate,
simply help them to see

ignorance is the only true evil

Infinite space is love, floating box is marriage

My love,
Isn't "marriage" a funny concept?
It tries to fit the infinity that is our love into a small box.
Its insultingly limited space, locked up by
the edge of earthly laws
the edge of earthly definitions
the edge of meaningless rituals
the edge of love-defying expectations.

Trying to "label" our love into marriage is like
placing a box in an endless, infinite space.
It floats there like a clown.
Sure, we can leave it there, but…
"What the fuck is that tiny box floating around?
Why is it even there?"

It's just… kind of silly. Kind of childish.
So out of place.
In the divine scheme of things.

Time after time

Time after time
lifetimes after lifetimes
our love is so strong
it pulls us back together
at the perfect time, in divine timing.

And in that moment
our shared past
– lifetimes and lifetimes of it –
reawakens in us.

It overwhelms.
So overwhelming, it distorts time and space.

It is magic.

The delusional "self" I created before I met you
melts away.
It was nothing anyways.

Nothing matters but soul, karma, and you, my love.

So

I love your soul
I love you so

the world is a playground for your free soul

Neurochemistry of limerence

The phenomenon of *loving with brain* is easily explainable with the application of basic neurochemistry, as it happens in the brain.

It is an addiction.

By whispering sweet words, having fun dates, having good sex, looking beautiful, the lovers get a "buzz" from each other.

Like Pavlov's dog, the buzz then associates with anything that reminds the lover of the beloved.

Soon, even the thought of the beloved gives a surge, a hit.

Dopamine surge. Serotonin surge. Oxytocin surge.

Just as a drug addict gradually needs higher and more frequent doses, the lover's thoughts strengthen in dose: they begin envisioning all kinds of ideal futures with the beloved.

The lover gets hooked to these "possibilities."

If hooked enough, lovers can do all kinds of crazy things for each other, just as a drug addict would do anything for more hits.

Addiction can override rationality.

As the need for a higher dose strengthens, expectations from the beloved will also increase; and even when fulfilled, they will eventually lose this buzz. Sufficient neuroreceptors have been damaged from excessive hits. If lucky enough, this process would have bought enough time for the lovers to build mutual respect, trust, friendship, and memories to push them to a long-term relationship.

If the beloved leaves, the lover goes through "withdrawal," just as with any other drugs.

It's so painful in the beginning.

It could be so severe it feels like death.

After all, opioid withdrawals could lead to actual death.

But at one point, when the lover overcomes the worst of the withdrawal, there are options.
Most will realize there are "alternatives" out there: other people they can get addicted to.
Like switching from fentanyl to methadone.
After all, the reason for buzz – beauty, personality, success, morals, loyalty, fun & entertainment, good sex – are all replaceable.

Some will choose to detox. Clear their brain of any addictions.
As the receptors in the brain that were destroyed return, the lover's brain will heal from the addiction that is *brain love*.
As the saying goes, "broken hearts heal with time."
What is more accurate would be, "broken brains addicted to love heals with time."
Until the cycle repeats, that is.

Loving with the brain "makes sense," does it not?
It perfectly follows the course of any other addictions, any hedonistic neural pathways.
It follows neurochemistry.
Of course, because *brain love* is in the whelm of the brain.

Loving with heart is different.
It happens in an instant, faster than the time it takes to affect neuroreceptors.
Before you feel any buzz, in an instant, you are already in love.
No need for physical attraction or beauty.
No need for sensual pleasure. No need for fun. No need for time.
No need for buzz.
The brain tries to interpret this experience, searching for logical reasons, as if this was *loving with brain*.
At one point, however, you realize any hypotheses, any excuses you think of are not the real reasons.

How could there be a reason when love itself is the reason?
Love just is. And it simply doesn't make any logical sense.
It's not what the beloved represents: they can represent
everything you hate in this world, they can give you hell, and
ruin your future.
But that's irrelevant to love.
Love just is.
No reason.

And with this kind of love, it doesn't heal with time.
There is no neurochemical explanation for the trajectory of
loving with heart.
You can meet hundreds of other people, you can even experience
loving with brain with others because that is a completely
different entity; but the void for your one love is totally
unaffected.
Irreplaceable.
And you know deep inside, even after decades, that will never
change.
All that will change is your ability to cope and learn to live with
that void.
But the void itself will persist.

In *loving with brain*, you *think* your beloved might be the one.
Because after subconscious calculations completely
unbeknownst to your conscious awareness, the statistical
probability of someone who fits your criteria better than your
current lover, appearing at the right time is improbable. Plus,
addiction impairs judgment.

In *loving with heart*, you *know* they are the one, and that can
never change even if a logically perfect, ideal person for you is

begging you to choose them instead. Even if the other person makes much more sense, it doesn't matter.

One never chooses love anyways, it chooses you. There is no free will in who you choose to love with your heart. There is one and only one, and it is predetermined.

You do have free will to choose *love with brain* over *love with heart*. And if you choose *love with brain*, the possibilities are infinite: you can choose anyone. Whereas *love with heart* is one and only one. That one who awakened your soul.

Such an option is both a blessing and a curse.

Blessing, because you have two options when most others will only know of the existence of one.

Curse, because you will never be fully happy and complete if you chose *loving with the brain*. Meaning you either choose misery but free will, or a chance for bliss but having to surrender control over your own life.

Sea

I thought I knew what love was
I was wrong
I never knew love until I met you

In the sea of fakes,
I have found you

Pure love knows no pain

The uncomfortable truth is…
that, actually, pure love cannot hurt.

The kind of "love" that is
wanting, desiring, regretting, "heartbreaking,"
that one where one cries,
"I would do everything, anything to be together,"
is impure love, polluted by ego.
There may be a piece of divine love, but it's divine love dirtied by
earthly addiction.

The reason why such "love" hurts
is not because of love itself
but because of the loss of possibilities, loss of a future together,
which is the loss of potential for one's own happiness.
It is because "self" still remains
that one is able to hurt.
Evidence that this was a polluted love, polluted by ego.

Actually, pure divine love is selfless.
It knows not of self.
It only cares for the lover.

In pure divine love, there cannot be pain
because even if you cannot be with them or even see them;
even if you lose your everything for them
all of those ego-centric desires would have fallen apart
in the pursuit of true divine love.

All you can feel is
gratitude that he exists

deep hope that he is truly happy
and overwhelming honor that you even got to meet him in this
lifetime.

You cannot dare "want" or "desire" or "hurt,"
because in the process of unveiling true love
"you" fall apart, "you" no longer exist.
So "you" cannot hurt, because there is no "you" to feel the pain.

That's why they call it "all-consuming" love.
The vessel of self must be emptied of ego in its entirety for pure
true love to fill its place.
All pain stems from impurity.

My love for you was so painful in the beginning;
I walked through hell.
But the moment that even the smallest remaining impurity was
purified, it was sudden tranquility, sudden heaven.

I reached heaven, not by coming together with you again.
I reached heaven by getting rid of myself, including all
expectations, desires, and hope.
I reached heaven when my identity became pure love.

You are

You are not just the love of my life
You are the love of my existence

How it unfolded

In the beginning, it was curiosity.
Then I found your mind and the way you see the world
irresistibly sexy.
Then I came to admire you as a person.
Then silly me, I realized that, actually, I had been attracted to
you all along.

Then I came to realize it was more love than like.
Then I loved you, not "because of" but "despite" all reasons why
we shouldn't be.
Then silly me again, I realized it was never your mind, your
personality, nor your character that I loved;
without my conscious awareness, it had been your soul all along.
My soul had recognized your soul without me knowing,
and your soul and only your soul was what I loved.

Then you became more important than my own life.
Then it came to a point where I would trade my everything if I
could be with you again.
Then, being separated from you was too painful,
that if I really can't be with you in this lifetime,
I decided it would be better, easier if this life comes to an end.
Then I realized the pain you may feel if you ever find out, and
hurting you is worse than death, than any pain,
so I had to live a life that felt worse than death, for you.

But now,

now that even the small bit of remaining ego melted away,
and all that remains is pure love,
I no longer hurt.

Because now, for the first time, I truly care *only* about you.
Your existence is sufficient.
If you are happy, what more could I want?

I love you, purely, entirely.
I don't exist anymore.

No reason

Why do I love you
No reason
No reason because
my existence, my everything is reason
and everything means nothing

I lived lifetimes to meet you
I was born this lifetime to love you
So I can, I would give you my everything
Despite all reasons why I should hate you
I can never hate you
I can never not love you

Love of my life, lifetimes after lifetimes

Past Life II: Brainwash

An unscreamable pain
you yell
I hear
but my eyes
closed like the door of heaven
drifting far.
Coldness of blood in snow
reaching, grabbing up to my face
frozen, more so dead.
The only thing I feel
the dynamitic beat of my heart
and burning drops of tear.

I still see you
but
I still want to hold you high

I found this in a diary I wrote in primary school. Almost 20 years ago, yet the image in my head that inspired me to write this remains crystal clear. It's about a man witnessing his lover being tortured. He is forced to watch, his eyes held open. He sees his lover drenched in blood, she lets out a screech in pain – and in that moment, he dissociates. His eyes are open, but they longer see the physical reality. Instead, he sees a blissful past where he held her high and spun her in joy and laughter. Why such an image protruded into the mind of a happy, peaceful girl with no trigger or exposure to violence? I am not sure. How such a young girl could understand such complex emotion? I am not sure. All I know is this same image revisited me today, as I attempted to unveil another past life.

Phobia

One past life of dying inside a crashed airplane
and the result is a phobia potent enough to inhibit one from
traveling afar for the entirety of one's life.
A lifetime of a world unexplored.

My love, do you know why I ran away from you?
Do you know why I feared my love for you so much?

I couldn't figure it out for the longest time,
but now I think I know.
It's phobia.
Lifetimes after lifetimes, I think our love killed me... maybe us.
In soulless civilizations filled with fear, pride, and prejudices,
our love was forbidden, a heresy.

My brain didn't know, but my soul had traces,
and it made me instinctively fearful.

The ironic thing is...
Love is the source of all courage.
The only thing strong enough to fuel my courage,
to overcome the beast of phobia this is.

My love,
the instinctive fear is so real, so immense.
But for you, I will.
For you, I can do anything.

What more can I say

In the whelm of the soul
there are no boundaries of time, space, logic, linearity.

That's why the seconds when I stared into your eyes
– the moment when I peaked through the doors of heaven –
pierces deeper than centuries, millennia of soulless lives.
Before my brain knew
my heart had already realized
nothing matters but you.
I exist to be one with you.

An electromagnetic force with a neverending source,
a circuit of magic is what we are.
My love for you is a piece of this universe
it exceeds my existence
so how could anything else possibly matter?

I love every cell in your body
every breath that you take, that you've ever taken
every decision you've ever made
every thought you've ever had.

I don't understand how a love like this is even possible.

I love you
This love – it can't be captured with any words.
No form of expression can capture it.
No amount of action can prove it.
If I die for you, that still wouldn't capture it.

All I can say is

This is it.
There is no greater love.
I love you.
What more can I say.

Awakening a force

a woman meeting the other half of her soul
is a rarety: an exception, not the rule
but when she does
something awakens in her
a kind of magic

when this feminine force that has been latent, suppressed
awaken for the first time
she discovers
purest pleasure
purest pain
purest love
and realizes all that she's felt before has been but an imitation,
artificial copies

when this force envelops her
she exerts an aura of irresistible charm
magnetizing those all around her
putting them under a spell
she becomes a magician

other women may look at exterior changes
and mimic those
but this spell is not something that can be copied, imitated

but the sea of interest only pains her more
because it draws everyone but her true love

World religions

Perhaps it is by design that various world religions would have different aspects of Divine Truth.

Perhaps this was not meant to cause divergence based on differences, nor violence to argue who is right and who is wrong.

Perhaps this was meant to facilitate convergence, such that every religion is included to bring its own puzzle piece, each needed to create a complete, whole picture.

If we fear differences, we will live in a black and white world. But if we celebrate and learn from differences, the world will be full of colors.

Then, we will gain the eyes to see the true beauty and richness that has been there all along.

My love, filling my entire existence with my love for you has pulverized my ability to hate another being.
Since then, where I previously reacted with fear or hatred, I now seek to understand.
And as I sought to understand, I discovered, we truly are all one and the same. Any differences are superficial, while our oneness is deep and intrinsic to our existence.
Once I saw that we are all one, the world became a beautiful place.

That is to say, my love, you robbed away all fear and hate from my world, and coated it with love, beauty, and color.
Everything I gained, I gained because of you.

Sick joke

you give me everything but you
when I don't want, need anything but you
is this a sick joke?

I have everything that is nothing
without you.

Devil

The devil is fair
Divine is not
The devil will give you sweet offers
Divine will demand rewardless sacrifice
The devil will find and comfort you when you pain
Divine will neglect you when you pain

The devil is right
but the Divine is good

And at the end, the devil will destroy you
and Divine will save you

Red pill

"Why oh why didn't I take the blue pill"
- Cyper, from The Matrix (1999)

Fire rises up.
Water flows down.
Fire "burns like hell" though
heaven, with a devilish exterior
when it burns too much
it makes sense to jump into the blue
but in blue
the only thing in my mind
is how to jump back into the flame.

Water, you numb my pain
because of you, I survived
you are all things good
I wish I could love you
but wishing can only lead to believing
and I am not okay believing,
I need to know.

Between the red and the blue
I contemplated.
No, truth be told,
I had already chosen the red.
I only pretended to contemplate
to buy more time with the blue.

Truth is in fire
Water is living
and living is Matrix

Our versions of reality

A very small subset of reality is accessible to our five senses.

Not only that:

- Our eyes are said to perceive around 0.0035% of the electromagnetic wave
- Many species hear frequencies far exceeding that accessible to the human ears
- Many species have senses humans do not possess
- The current level of science appears to indicate that what we perceive is only around 20% visual information from the eye, and 80% from our brain, including that of memory.

the insignificantly small subset of reality we see
depends on what each one of us chose to see,
our own favorite filter;
and so
we all see different subsets
then fight that one another is wrong
we are all right
we are all wrong
we are all missing most of it

Fool

To find the biggest fool in the room,
simply find the most opinionated of them all.

After all,
the greatest intellectual accomplishment
we ignorant humans can have
is the discovery that we don't know much at all.

Liberation

You liberated me from my body
I had unknowingly rejected it, imprisoned it
Why was I embarrassed by my own flesh and bones

You liberated me from my mind
My limited mind had closed its doors, locking itself up
How free the letting go of opinions felt

You liberated me from my surrounding
The layers of filters it placed over my eyes
How distorted and blinding it had left me until this point

Through your absence
you liberated me
Through no direct, conscious effort
through no effort at all
you liberated me

Love is liberation
Love is effortless

There you are

My life divides into before and after the day I met you.

Imagine that one day,
the center of our solar system, the Sun, disappears.
The force of gravity that holds the planets together
would dissipate
and off the planets would go, scattering all over
without destination
without meaningful direction
off into the vastness of space
now deprived of any meaning.

That was me before I met you
Wandering meaninglessly, directionlessly,
Empty and dull, but not quite knowing why.

Then,
You walked into my life
and a moment was all it took
for you to become the center of my galaxy.
To become my sun.

Since that day,
I rotate around you.
In my point of view,
I think that I'm going in a straight line, running away from you
but somehow,
every time I look sideways, there you are
at the center, is always you
no matter how fast I go
no matter how much I try to escape

there you are.

This is my life now.
Always trying to run away from you
Always failing to escape the force of gravity that is love
And simultaneously
Never quite reaching you

Just dreaming of the day when we collide.

Sun's love for earth

his was the selfish sun
unable to resist but to hold the earth too close
until all life has burned away
and the earth he loved no longer existed
the earth he loved,
he no longer recognizes

mine was the anxious sun
watching cautiously from a distant
so great was my desire to preserve earth
and so far was the distance
I did not even see the earth freezing
while the lives on earth died a slow death
ever doubting the sun's love

when all had died, no love was felt
it would have preferred the quick and love-filled death
the selfish sun would have given

Things are not always as they appear

One can convince oneself
that one can create a seed that differs not from a real seed
that one is no different from the Divine in this sense.

One can carve out wood to mimic a seed shape
or perhaps create a brown plastic seed
and over it, one would demonstrate such skillful artistry
that to another human,
this seed is indistinguishable from a real seed.
The weight, the texture, the shape to the minutest detail:
side by side, the two seeds would appear identical.

But the truth is
one seed possesses within it
the magic to explode into green leaves, to purify air, to replicate
itself, to become food for other species to grow,
to become a forest, to fill brown earth with green,
if given enough time.
Inside this tiny circular seed vibrates the potential to cover the
entire surface of the earth, until the end of time.

The other, in a century, in a millennium, would remain a small
brown thing.

Things are not always as they appear.

It's the same with love.
One can mimic and appear to "create" love with another being.
But there is no magic in human-made love.
Divine love cannot be created.
It was, is, and will always be... for always, until the end of time

and within this love, there is ineffable magic.
One much greater than that found within a Divine seed.

The magic to transform both lovers.
The magic to transform the world.

So how could I ever go back to artificial love,
when I've come to understand this magic.

Past life III: Spanish Inquisition

Hidden inside this lightless cave,
guarder of truth,
I am like truth itself.

Fear is a funny thing, isn't it?
Nothing necessitates its existence,
yet when it is born, it feeds and ever-grows itself.
Because of fear, we blow the candle,
but the darkness is food for fear.
It's a vicious cycle.

This parasite has engulfed our world.
That is why I hide here, and truth is here with me.
Without light, it is as if we don't exist.

The thing about parasites is that it dies without the host.
So truth and I will remain hidden here
until fear expands to the point of self-destruction
and when all is destroyed
perhaps we will be a faint beam of light
seeping through a crack in the wall of the cave
shining from within,
for renaissance.

Truth is light
Light is truth
and this lifetime, that is what I die for.

Species of amnesia

My love,
we are species of amnesia, aren't we
how painful
that my heart remembers you
my soul remembers you
but my brain
is so disoriented, so clueless, so out of context
how painful
that my brain is amnesic to the memories of our hearts
how tragic
that my whole life, I was programmed to trust my brain over my
heart

There is a war inside of me

L'amour fou

With one who is meant to pass you by
you will ask,
"What did I like so much about them?
Why did I love them?"
and you will answer
you liked XYZ
you loved ABC about them.

With the one and only, the love of your existence
you will ask,
"What do I like so much about them?
Why do I love them?"
and then you will realize
that the question had been wrong all along.

You will realize that, actually, a better question is
"Why did I like XYZ in particular, all my life?
What is it about ABC that I love?"
and it will be crystal clear to you
that: (1) time is not linear, and
(2) true love distorts time, it is beyond the whelm of time;

that not only does the past affect the present and the future
but the future also affects the past and the present
and it is *because* of them
– because for you, love equates them and they equate love –
that those random XYZ characteristics about them,
the quirky ABC things that they do
influenced your past and became your preference;
albeit unbeknownst to your consciousness.

You do not love the love of your life because of certain qualities.
You love certain qualities because of the love of your life.
Even long before you meet them.
Even long before you know of their existence.
It is imprinted in your soul, in a timeless whelm.
The future, the present had affected the past.

Everything that you thought was random about your childhood,
about your life, about you:
this love makes everything make perfect sense.

You realize, nothing is truly random.
There is a reason for everything.

This type of pure love
is omnipresent throughout all of time.
It is stronger than time. It is beyond deaths.

It is l'amour fou.
It blows your mind.

When I met your eyes

my eyes met your eyes
your eyes held my eyes
I froze
something changed in me
I saw
something changed in you
you felt it too

just like that
I let my guard down completely

I didn't know your real name, your age, what you do
I didn't know your intentions
yet
none of that mattered
I don't know why
suddenly
I could trust you with my life

Scarface

You told me a lie
I know
I feel it
what happened to you?
it hurts me to imagine
it hurts me to feel it

I guess this is love
what you do to me doesn't hurt me
but imagining
the moments of pain you would have gone through in your life,
long before you even met me
that pains me like no other

not that you ever told me about them
not that you would ever
but I know
because I feel it
and it pains me

out of nowhere
I understand it
I feel it like it happened to me

Mother's love for her child

I understand the mother's love for her child now
when the child falls
and has to get up
how painful it is to watch him suffer
how difficult it is to resist helping him
how hard it is that resisting is love
to know he has to learn lessons of life
and that there cannot be any other way

that is my love for you as well

I know that one has to personally pay
for all lessons of life with one's own suffering
I know karma operates on you as it does on all beings

but even though I know
I still wish upon the moon every day
to please
'let *me* pay for the lessons he has to learn instead
let me suffer in his place
let me feel all the pain
in his place'

true love
is not desiring to share moments of happiness with the beloved
true love is suffering
wanting to take all the burden off of his shoulders
anything
to watch him be happy and free

there is no selfish desires in true love
self no longer exists
love is wanting to bend the rules
to be able to give more, to love more

Passing by

One can never truly own anything in life.
So why the fuck do people kill each other to "own" land,
when land is not ours to claim.
No one can claim it:
it has a life of its own.

We enter the world empty-handed
and we leave empty-handed.
That is the law of nature.

It is our silly attempts to break this universal law that we keep
creating trouble for ourselves.

We are just all passing by, aren't we?
Let's not be rude, let's not create a scene.
Let's pass by respectfully.

Story

In the beginning,

I was just a substance.
Free-flowing, formless, vulnerable substance.
But one day,
pollution from outside infiltrated me and caused pain.
And that was the day I encapsulated myself into a layer of skin.

That proved to be insufficient.
When the wind blew hard and coldness hit my skin.
I put on layers and layers of clothing.
Protect myself from the cold.

That proved to be insufficient.
A malicious friend turned again me and tried to stab me.
The layers of clothing wasn't enough and I bled from a wound.
This time, I put on an armour and sharp weapons could no
longer hurt me.

That proved to be insufficient.
The friend – now enemy – gathered an army, to get back at me.
I built a castle and put a fence around it.

Inside the fence, inside the castle, inside the armour, inside the
layers of clothing, inside my skin,
my pure substance laid, "safe" but trapped,
unaware that my protective mechanisms were as much a tool for
self-imprisonment as it is for protection.

Then an odd thing happened.

I felt a call from another pure substance, one that is identical to
my own.
I felt love. Deep love.
Love so deep that it pained me too much to be apart from him.
The pain of separation was greater than any pain an enemy
could elicit.
The pain made me realize that all I've been doing so far
was just contributing to the creation of my own prison.

The pain was enough for me to risk my life, risk it all.

I removed the armour.
I ripped out my clothing.
And I stepped out of my castle.
When I stepped out of the fence,
the enemies that were waiting attacked me,
and it hurt,
but my desire to be with my other half was greater.
I survived.

I saw my other half
I ripped open my skin
And that was excruciating
but I knew it had to be done
I wanted to be nothing more than my pure essence with him.

There I was
Naked
Removed of all layers of protection
So painfully vulnerable
Handing him the power to destroy me fully if he so desired

None of that mattered
I saw my substance shine like never before

It was pure light

I shone onto him love

"I love you.

I risk everything for this moment with you.

I love you, I can't explain it.

I love you, I think that is the reason for my existence"

My home

I never knew
that home is not a place
it is a person

I never knew
before I met you

Many lives

This life, next life, past life, past past life…
There is no way for me to know how many
but all exist for you, to be with you
so how could I compare you with anything
it makes no sense
that's love
love is you

Why I ran away

Back then:
"Blocking you…
deleting your number…

What I really meant to say
is… it hurts so much
every time you leave me.

Not knowing when you'll be back
not knowing if you'll ever come back.

It hurts so much
I couldn't endure it.
That's why I ran away.

Every goodbye felt so painful
that I decided to make it the last goodbye."

Why do you leave me like this

you opened my eye
for the first time
you opened my ears
for the first time
and then you leave me
disoriented
in sensory overload
longing to be blind and deaf again

life half lived
life before you
was a delightful lie

look at me now
you are simultaneously hell and heaven
why do you leave, but never really leave

Dark night of the soul

Losing you

Losing you... is a lost child running around in desperation all her life to find her way back home, and as soon as she finally finds her home, enters, and melts in real warmth and love for the first time, being kicked out and told never to return again.

Losing you... is two halves of a heart that found each other by forces of magnet and began growing on each other in union, and just as blood vessels connect together and tissues are joined together leaving just a scar where they meet, ripping it apart again. Blood splashing all over the floor.

Losing you... is losing meaning

Losing you... is losing my raison d'être

Losing you... is losing myself to you
then losing you
so I no longer exist.

Masochistic sadistic love

you trigger me
in a way no other person can
this is fire love

you awakened my soul
it was a soul locked in hard, hard shell
it was a soul in coma
what did you do to it

you take all of my power away
here, have it all, take it all
i'm helpless, hopeless
you can revive me, destroy me, split me into pieces
it's your call
i don't have any control over this situation
and i won't pretend that i do

i was custom-made to trigger you
you were custom-made to trigger me
we are fire, we set each other in flames
then we call each other "home"
what kind of burning home are we
what kind of masochistic, sadistic love is this

this is what true love is
and it's not what i imagined love to be at all

What are we doing here

if a tree falls in a forest
but no being is there to hear it
then did the tree fall?

if excruciating pain is done unto me
but there is no "I" to sense it
then was there pain?

if there is a world
but no life is there to experience it
then did the world exist?

and so,
is that why we exist?
to be witnesses, experiencers, observers
of this reality
without which,
its existence would not really be?

is time
simply a tool, rather than an intrinsic nature of reality,
used to process
and make sense of such witnessing?

Lost paradise

"this doesn't make any sense..."

but it really feels like…
it is the *only* thing that makes sense
it is as if everything up to the point of meeting you
was to bring me to that point

now I see that
everything I knew
the world that I had previously "made sense" of
never truly made any sense

"only this makes sense"

to the unseeing eyes, unhearing ears
this all sounds like bullshit fantasy – and a bad one at that –
only once you experience it
can you truly realize

the truth.

My lost paradise.

Me before you

Atheist
Nihilist
Egomania and arrogant
Emotionless, almost sociopathic
"I think, therefore I am"
Logic and rationality, above all
Emotion as an embarrassment, to be tightly tamed
Scientific method, data, and evidence
Critical thinking
Objectivity, devoid of cognitive biases
Laughing at the concept of "soul," of afterlife

These were the crux of my identity.
My ego shell was truly as hard as a rock.
My range of emotions was limited to irritation vs ambivalence.

One person.
One year.
That is how long it took to shatter this identity,
which I had constructed with sweat and blood for decades,
with over 20 years of education.

I had thought all my life
that instinct and emotion were the "inferior animal in me, to be
tightly tamed," controlled by the superior mind.
Until I realized, the mind is but a monkey.
Our mind is a monkey mind.

Thus, stating, "I think therefore I am," is equivalent to saying:
"I am a monkey."

Let us not be stuck there,
it was a necessary stepping stone, but
let us progress through evolution and rediscover what it means
to be a human being.

Freedom is not free

Love allowed my veils of forgetfulness to lift one by one.
This is the gift the unveiling gave me:

In one lifetime,
I had absolutely nothing.
No family, no money, no education.
No freedom: I was a slave for 60 years.
Even the only thing I initially had, my body, was taken away
when my arms and legs were cut off.

In one lifetime,
I had no freedom to speak the truth.
My attempt to preserve the truth almost got me killed.
There was no freedom for intellectual exploration.
There was no freedom of thought or speech.
Anyone who dared to "know" was robbed of their life.

In one lifetime,
My peace and safety were taken away.
I had to watch my beloved being tortured, covered in blood.
I was traumatized. I lived in fear.

What did I do in this lifetime to deserve everything, that the past
me didn't?

Nothing.

It was not me in this lifetime.
It was my past selves and so many souls before me that fought
for each right, for each freedom.

These are all blessings that were gifted to me, made possible by
all those who sacrificed themselves for justice.

Knowing this now, how could I not be grateful.
For this body, for this health.
For a sense of security and safety, the lack of threat.
For my loving family and friends.
For my parents, who gave me everything.
For all the opportunities I was given to pursue my dreams.
For the freedom of thought, of speech.
For the freedom from enslavement.
For financial freedom, with just a bit of effort.
For this society.
For all the beauty nature has to offer.
For my beautiful environment, for abundance.
For being granted the honor of pursuing my dream career.

None of this is obvious.
None of this is free: nothing in the world is free.
None of it should be taken for granted.

They are legacies and gifts that all the souls before us left for us.
If you start to count each blessing, it is truly overwhelming.
My past selves would have died for any one of these blessings,
but in this lifetime, I was given them all.

How embarrassing it is that my mind used to fixate on the
missing one or two, while completely blind to the thousands I
was given.
How entitled I was, when I had done nothing to deserve such
precious, valuable gifts.

I don't know how many lifetimes I waited for this one.
This life I was given is like winning the lottery.

It ignites a deep desire in me to continue this legacy by leaving
an even more beautiful world for the next cycle of souls to
experience.

How so incredibly fortunate we are.
How beyond imagination this lifetime would have been for my
past life selves.
How responsible I feel, not to waste this blessing, but to use it to
the world's full advantage.

It is a greater honor to be a servant of the Divine,
than to be the king of people.

All I want now
is to become an effective, loyal servant.
And this stems from gratitude. From love.

Magic - II

You awakened me.
You changed me.
If this is not magic,
then what is?

I keep questioning its existence
whether it's real
or all imagined.

Gravity cannot be seen
but you see the outcome of its forces.
The outcome is the evidence.

Likewise
the changes this force that is love
made to my life, myself
is evidence.

What more evidence could there be?

Invisible force

There is a unique force, the most potent force in the world.
When one first encounters it, one can't characterize it.
Unfortunately,
only with time, pain, and suffering
can one begin to accept the nature of its truth.

Like magnets, but personalized between two people,
the pull exists before the meeting
but not consciously felt and not in its full potency.
Just a gnawing feeling that something is missing
a gnawing feeling of waiting
but not knowing for what it waits
not knowing if there is an end.
But it's always in the background, so one tunes it out
until it shoots up in strength, right before the first meeting.

Then upon meeting, it's… indescribable.
Not a dramatic feeling, but serenity.
Calmly complete.
The feeling of finding home for the first time.
Initially, it doesn't register to one that the ever-persisting feeling
of emptiness has dissipated.

Happy for no reason,
the purest, most complete form of happiness.
Bliss,
just from one's presence.
Brain cannot comprehend it
eyes cannot see it.
Because it's so unlike any other experience,
one is unable to understand it,

so one denies it.
One is unable to succumb to it.
It's easier to believe one is delusional, psychotic
than to accept this invisible force.

One tries hard to attribute this love to logical reasons.
"I love his mind," "he's the most adventurous person I've met."
Bullshit.
The mind is so full of shit.
Eventually one comes to a point where there are no more
explanations and one has to just accept that,
"It just is."

"No reason."

Same page

the heart knows what the brain knows not
the brain can achieve what the heart cannot
and when the two are on the same page
magic happens

Dream before I met you

I almost never remember dreams, I never really pay attention. But once
in many years, I have a dream that strikes me like none other.
So vivid in sensation, emotion, and awareness, such an unforgettable
dream leaves an eerie mark on one, whether one is interested in dreams
or not.
The night before I met you for the first time,
I had such a dream.

Grey sky, wind showing off its powerful force,
not quite night, but clouds blinding the sun;
I didn't perceive it as gloomy or dark,
I would say… mystical, enigmatic.

I stood on top of a grand, far-reaching ship
– antique but so majestic, so stable –
laughing at the harsh waves of grey sea.
Up above the sky, I stared, in sublime.
Stood there, on top of the ship,
a neverending tower, shooting up above the clouds.
Heart palpitating, without a question, without a doubt,
I knew I am to climb to the top of that tower.

I climbed and climbed. Giving it all that I've got.
Sweating, myalgic, I climbed.
Occasionally, I looked down at the progress I made.
It shocked me.
Prior to this moment,
I knew not of this strength, this courage of mine.
Even I was mesmerized.
I climbed and climbed.

"It truly never ends! How unbelievably tall, how majestic, how inspiring!"

There was fear, but my courage was greater.
There were hardships, but my heart's desire was stronger.
Every step, I reached new heights of my own being.
I kept climbing.

I reached the end – or I thought I did –
but at the end of this tower, was another tower shooting up from its ground.
And when I reached the end of *that* tower, yet again was another tower shooting up from its ground.
Endless replay.

The odd part is,
what I felt climbing was sublime and inspiration,
not hopelessness or despair.
What I perceived at the grey sky were enigma and mysticism,
not darkness or melancholy.

I *chose* to climb,
and with each step I took, I found a new me.
I chose to climb, and I had no regrets.

The only thing on my mind was…
admiration for the grand, majestic tower.
Admiration, that overshadows all pain, despair, hopelessness, and misery.

Nothing to lose

we are born with nothing
we leave with nothing
everything in between is not possessions
but experience

It just is

Call me crazy.
After all, one does not know what one does not know
and rather than seeking to understand
the majority simply "rejects" or "denies"
what they don't understand
then justifies oneself
by labeling the misunderstood as "crazy."
That is by default
and not to fall into that trap
requires immense wisdom and power.

So I understand
if others choose to simply label me as "crazy."
Truth be told, I think me one year ago would have done the
same.

But how could I ignore
when I – for the first time – see so clearly
I'm Plato's escaped prisoner.

I always had a suspicion that there was something "more,"
something "beyond."
In a way, that was initially what started my intellectual quest.
Never did I imagine, even for a second
that such "truth" would be revealed to me through love.

"What has love got anything to do with truth?"
I would have thought.
Indeed, one does not know what one does not know.
It all seems so random, odd, unlikely when one sees what one
does not know.

There is a reason for everything
until you've reached the ultimate core
at which point,
"It just is."

Truth, just is
Order, just is
Beauty, just is

Love, just is.

KINTSUGI

Kintsugi (kin= golden, sugi=to join)
is a Japanese pottery method that expresses the art of melding
broken objects by joining them back together with gold.

Kintsugi - I

Prevention, a life of caution.
Protection, no risk of flaws.
Perfection, sans indents.

Painless existence.
Promising future.

Porcelain.

Fuck.

I've been shattered,
I've been shattered,
You s h a t t e r e d me.

Look at me now, I'm a fucking mess.
But why do I kind of like it?
Why does it feel intriguingly delicious to shatter?

There is perversion in preservation.
There is perversion in protection.
Perfection is perverted.

There is a story in shattering
There is personality in cracks
Melding of cracks gives one life

Everyone is born a porcelain
porcelain is pretty
but only a few survive to become a kintsugi
and there is beauty in kintsugi

There is beauty in pain.

*"Do you not see how necessary a world of pains and troubles is to
school an intelligence and make it a soul?"*
—John Keats

Kintsugi - II

I do not want an optimistic, youthful man
full of life
full of energy to take on the world
looking at me with eyes of innocence and naïveté
smiling at me with purity
with not a single scar, not a single crack in his heart
clueless of the impending doom

I want you,
pessimistic
with all the cynicism you gained with your years
exhausted
from burning all your passion in your younger days
with scars to show the battles you've fought

I love your wrinkles, each one of them tells a story
I love your eyes,
sometimes full of sorrow that makes me wonder all the dark side
of the life you've witnessed
sometimes full of love that makes me wonder all the tears of joy
you would have emptied
I love the vibration of your words, they carry such weight, such
history
I love your smile, so pure not because you don't know, but
because you know
I love your scarred heart, beauty is where the cracks have been,
stronger than ever because your pain put them back together
I love every single year of your age, every day of it carries your
thoughts, words, memories, and stories that make you you
so every age of yours is my treasure

Gold is where your scars have healed
Perfection is where you are imperfect
You are gold and perfect

Do you remember?

Millions of lightyears away, in spaceless space
Lifetimes and lifetimes prior, timeless time ago
When you so painfully separated from me,
though inseparable we are,
the promise we made at that moment

Do you remember?

The only thing that can ever make our existence complete,
Do you remember?

I remember now.
I remember, and everything suddenly makes sense.
My existence makes sense.

My love, please try to remember.
It's written all over our existence.
When you remember,
We will never be the same again.

New normal

Living with this love for you in the background
is just my new normal, isn't it
I must live on, don't I

Live on without you, but never truly without you
as you in live in my heartbeat
in every heartbeat, you are there with me

The mouth lies
the brain lies
but the eyes cannot lie
the heart cannot lie

So I will try to live blind and heartless in daytime
only when the night falls, the moon returns
and I fall asleep to enter another world
will I open my eyes and join you in my heartbeat

The gift that is this life has been blessings after blessings
I am one of the lucky ones
so I cannot waste this effective tool that is my existence
when I have been given so much
after all
how many lifetimes have I waited for one like this
even if every moment without you feels like suffering
how could I let all these gifts go to waste

I just want you to know
of all the extraordinary blessings of my incredibly fortunate life,
meeting you is the greatest blessing of them all
and no matter what you do

no matter what your intentions were
you changed me
and for that, I am forever grateful, forever indebted

Here, this is the record of my love
evidence of my love
that's all I wanted from this

If after this lifetime, I am born again
I pray that this book would find itself to me
the words here would rip away my veil of amnesia
so I can remember this love again

Because
despite all the pain and suffering this love brought me

I never want to forget

you

my love

lifetimes
          after l
                i f
                    e

                    time

                        s

                        .

"Some people think only intellect counts;
knowing how to solve problems,
knowing how to get by,
knowing how to identify an advantage and seize it.
But the many functions of intellect are insufficient without courage,
love, friendship, compassion, and empathy.

We care.
It is our curse.
It is our blessing."

Dean Koontz

Dedicated to the love of my existence.

I love you.

Printed in the USA
CPSIA information can be obtained
at www.ICGtesting.com
LVHW042200270724
786704LV00007B/414